As Sweet As It's Going To Get

As Sweet As It's Going To Get

poems

Dawn Coppock

Dawn Coppock

Sapling Grove Press
www.saplinggrovepress.com

Copyright © 2015 by Dawn Coppock.

All rights reserved. No part of this publication may be reproduced, distributed, or transmitted in any form or by any means, electronic or mechanical, without written permission from the publisher, Sapling Grove Press, except for brief quotations in articles, books, and reviews, or for educational purposes.

Publisher's web site: www.saplinggrovepress.com.

Library of Congress Cataloging-in-Publication Data
Coppock, Dawn, (1962 --   )
As Sweet As It's Going To Get, poems, motherhood, marriage and divorce, adoption, rural life, Dawn Coppock.

ISBN 978-0-692-35810-8

Cover photograph, *In Dawn's Kitchen,* 2014 © by David underwood; used by permission from the artist. Visit: www.underwoodartworks.com.

Manuscript edited by Susan O'Dell Underwood.
Book text font and cover font is Optima.
Book and cover design by David Underwood.
Interior pie photographs © by David Underwood.
The actual apple pie in these pictures was made by Dawn Coppock. (Yes, we did actually get to eat the pie while working on this book.)
The author's personal web site is: www.dawncoppock.com.

Author photograph © by Leo Coppock-Seal.

Printed in the United States of America.
First Edition, January 2015.

This book is dedicated to Audrey and Leo Coppock-Seal.

Table of Contents   **Page**

Poetry	11
Billing Hourly	13
Reconstruction	14
Cooking in the New South	17
Road Flowers	18
We Weren't Married Yet	19
Soaking in Pontassieve	20
Longing of a Girl Long Married	21
Now She Strains Against the Lashings	22
A Diamond is the Hardest Thing in the World	23
Understatement	24
The Coffee Is Cold	25
Noritake Magnificence #9736	26
Blood is Green	27
July Communion	28
Undertow	29
Working Mother	31
Naming Women	32
At the Lorraine Motel	36
Leo's Magic Pillow at the Fourth of July Picnic	37
Dancing	38
Star Wars	39
On Being Loved By Leo	40
Waking to Violins	41
View From the Buggy	42
She Thinks I'm Hard	43
At Eleven	44
The Size of Sadness	45
Options for an Unplanned Pregnancy	46
Cross Your Legs, Sweetheart	48
Photographs of Startled Men at McDonald's	49

Revised Standard Version 50
Waiving Grace 51
Returning Joshua 52
Two Daughters Have Breakfast 53
Mourning Prayer 54

Rx: Dirty Socks 55
Old Testament Man 56
Be Bigger Than Me 57
Regeneration 58
Upon Meeting an Old Lover 59
Winter Communion 60
Two by Two 61

[Let me wander through just one day] 63
Advice from a Blue Heron 64
Praise With Joy 65
The Nature of Light 66
October on the Tennessee-North Carolina State Line 68
To Hold 69
Small Game 70
Walking the Farm Without You 71
Statement of Faith 72

[Time] 75

Acknowledgments 77

Poetry

You get a lot more words
for your money
with a novel.

Billing Hourly

My wife puts up fruit.
She's one of those lady lawyers.
They's about thirty-five dollars'-worth of jelly
on this here biscuit.

Reconstruction

I never heard my mama say she was from Alabama.
But when the will was read and the land divided,
the land was in Alabama.
Mama doesn't fry chicken.
She bakes it,
with orange marmalade and Lipton's onion soup mix.

My daddy so loathed his childhood sustenance,
he drew back, scorched
when he saw his mama's Fiesta Ware in my cabinet.
Beans and cornbread, turnips, deviled eggs --
toxic waste on rainbow plates.

Mama escaped fried chicken.
Daddy escaped pimento cheese.
Escaped and took us with them
to B.A. and B.S. and M.S. and damn near Ph.D.
Rancher ranches,
sanitized, sterilized, starched and pressed,
mid-America, South.

"Mezrez Lindsay! I got Mezrez Lindsay."
"Her name is not *Mezrez* anything!"
"But Mama, that's what she told us her name is."
"*You'll* not call her that. No child of mine. . .
Jim! Jim, I told you we never should have left Atlanta."

Appalachia,
a geography word.
Like plateau, hemisphere, continental divide. . .
I lived in the Appalachian hemisphere,
or the Appalachian time zone?

At twelve, I found "Old Blue," "Wagoner's Lad,"
and "Who's Gonna Shoe My Pretty Little Foot"

on hiccuppy vinyl at the library.
Then, at an all-day singing, I found the people.

They ate boiled turnips
with oily butter floating in droplets
and clinging to the edges of each white chunk.
I thought they were potatoes, at first.
They slyly watched me with this rough old food.
I was just happy to have found the foundation,
the precise location and shape of my connection to this earth.
I could rebuild.

I got the apple stack cake recipe from Aunt Rose.
Biscuits and sausage gravy
from a two-year tour of duty at Hardee's.
Handwork, posthumously,
from Aunt Goldie's sugar sack pillowcases.
Vinegar on greens and just in general from Mamaw Coppock.
Creamed corn, Canasta and calling a spade a spade
from Aunt Ina.
Who not to call a spade from Papaw Coppock.
Sun Drop and moonshine, the celestial cocktail, in Tullahoma.
And molasses from sticky Mason jars
bought Over Home from dusty, hard-eyed boys
for whom this is as sweet as it's going to get.

At seventeen I found a hairy man who got dirty at work
to shoe my pretty little foot.
He helped with the finish work.
He gave me how to drive a tractor on a hill,
and "Man, I heard that."
Pinto beans as the staff of life from his mama.
Chow-chow, pessimism and cat gravy from Blanch.
And "Those cedars'll take the place" from Beldon.

We bought the old Doane farm at auction.
"God, were people living here when you bought this place?"
My people, it turned out.
Much later, a tug on a genealogical thread revealed
Susan Ann Doane, my great, great grandmother
in the chain of title.
Oblivious, I'd bought the family farm,
right down to white enamel chamber pots in the chicken house.
Cellular destiny.

It skipped a generation.
But here I am
sleeping under a tin roof
with my Renaissance redneck,
buying pinto beans in the economy size.

Cooking in the New South

There's balsamic vinegar for the greens.
Three Rivers cornbread,
a golden inhalation in a cast iron pan,
is timed on the microwave.
A 6-inch pan is plenty.
I've got the pill.

There is no lard. Bits of country ham
from a freezer zip bag.
No time to trim a hunk off a hog.
But the fried okra is legendary,
and the biscuits are as light
as the ghosts in this kitchen.

Road Flowers

"Chigger weeds," he says,
"that's all I ever
heard them called."

I walk toward him,
arms full,
my light and lacy trousseau.
"I never heard that," I say.

"Are you taking those in the house?"

In a vase,
"Queen Anne's Lace."

"I never heard that," he says.
"What's your favorite flower?"

"Road flowers," I say.

He smiles and shakes his head.

His Poorland Daisy my Black-eyed Susan,
his Tickseed my Coreopsis,
Horseweed my Chicory.
Daisy
Honeysuckle
Wild rose

Queen Anne's Lace.
He's heard it now.
My lacy white gift brought into this house.

We Weren't Married Yet

Funny how that makes the memory more romantic.
We were poor then, and rented the shed
in the yard of a rambling, white beach house.

Two rusty springs poked through the dirty mattress.
I taped brown paper bags over them,
and we lolled there anyway
until Halley's Comet was due.

When we slipped on to the deck of the big house,
he had a steel thermos of hot black coffee.
I had the kangaroo pocket of my sweat jacket
full of Little Debbie oatmeal pies.

A lovers' picnic
by the moonslicked sea.
It was too cold to stay out long,
and the comet was smaller than we expected.

Soaking in Pontassieve

Lying back in a deep, old tub,
me in Chianti, Chianti in me,
my breasts float as the Arno curves
against the hills. April pours
through wooden shutters, eyelids, pores.

In love in a country that doesn't do
bathrooms in peach and pink, seashells and roses.
Here, terra cotta, plaster and brass.
The outside flows in, leaving only sky
blue, cypress, and silver green.

Here, where there is no love
without romance and all the wine
has corks.

The plug is pulled.
Dizzy and warm
we make love for the gnarly old olive trees,
twisted rubber bands
that when turned loose will spin this world
like unfurling the belly button of God.

Longing of a Girl Long Married

Love me, not
with the proven tricks
of a thousand tangled nights.

Touch my wrist in the kitchen
and ask to press your fingers
to the deep softness of my breast.

It's the absence of asking
that makes marriage hard,
loss of the wondering
what I might say.

Now She Strains Against the Lashings

She tried ballooning but the sky was too big.
The storms scared her.
She shivered up high.
She might be lost.
By twenty-three she wanted to rest,
to bob a bit at tether.

So when he came to her, shoulders laden
with great coils of rope, she welcomed him
and shunned those offering just hot breath.

A Diamond is the Hardest Thing in the World

Each day I jam on the rings of engagement
and marriage.
His charms of protection, like garlic
around my neck.

Understatement

Imagine one day your husband woke up
and said, "I'm sorry, darling, you were right
about everything. I don't see how
you stood it all those years. I'll be
different from now on. I'm different already."
And that day, anyway, he was.

Imagine it was more insight
than he had shown in eighteen years.
That you would have sooner expected
your cat to cook a five course meal.
But now you know that the cat could cook all along
and just wouldn't be bothered.

Imagine you had planned your life without him
and you were looking forward to it.
That you thought anyone
who would trust that man again
should have "Stupid" tattooed on her forehead.
Imagine he was still handsome
and the father of your children.

Imagine you are in an action adventure.
The garage door is closing.
You are supposed to dive under.
But instead -- you hesitate,
wishing he had stayed a bastard.
Wishing you knew just what to do next.

The Coffee Is Cold

I want to scream, "You are not cute!"
when you stretch and grin
and scratch your nuts at 11 a.m.
It would have been cute at 7 or 8
or before you made me pregnant
twice, but now the Cheerios have dried
to the sides of the bowls.
It's 5 loads of laundry past sun up,
and you are not cute at all.

Noritake Magnificence #9736

      I

I can't even remember the girl-bride
who liked these little white butterflies,
the way the art deco angles and bars
are softened by mauve and pink roses.

Wedding dishes don't go
with a Chinese red dining room.
They can't live in a cabin or on a house boat.
They won't serve
cornbread or baked tofu.
There's a canape dish, for God's sake.

Eighteen years, trapped
under the gilded lid
of a dainty little sugar bowl.
That curly vine encircling the plates
I thought was so romantic
has twisted around my ankle.

      II

In the divorce I got the china
we'd both forgotten.
I opened the top cabinet and found it,
unexpected, like the toothbrush of someone
who died in a wreck.
Dishes cocooned between circles of white felt
I cut out years before.

Please just fall. Splinter on yourselves,
plates upon cups, saucers upon bowls,
shatter a shining circle around me.
But the china didn't fall. It waited for me,
like the years I spent wishing
that he would have an affair.

Blood is Green

The day a man gets a new bass boat,
that's Royal Blue,
and a toddler in a twirly dress, always Yellow.

The day your daddy has a stroke, Orange
like a hunting vest.

Red roses from the florist,
the ones that don't smell,
they are Muddy Brown.

But good dirt is Green,
like that little hike up Laurel Falls,
hot or cold,
always Green,

that pushy, mossy, springy Green.
Alive, it screams,
in a voice that Red
can't even dream.

July Communion

On this farm, the first blackberry is not
eaten alone. *Two or three gathered*
for me is a son and a daughter.

Hip deep in weedy mystery,
hot, living wine -- taken together,
unearned gifts sublime, a son and a daughter.

Stickers snag bloody streaks along our arms.
Transubstantiation. A son
and a daughter. *This do in remembrance.*

Undertow

In this dream I am hugely pregnant,
yet insubstantial.
Under thin permeable skin
my bones are chalk,
like the bones of canned fish.

Eyes averted, we move gingerly
through jostling elbows, distorted faces.
Blasts of laughter and chatter
dissolve us
like splashes on reflection.

Hands splayed
around my belly, we seek sanctuary,
but the crowd has no edges.
Heedless, they would crush us
like shells underfoot.

I cannot safeguard
another one.
It's just too hard. I fear
it is impossible,
like singing under water.

Working Mother

I have been shot
from a circus cannon.
In arching freefall,
I hurtle toward earth.

I ought not whine about
having everything

Naming Women

    I.

Dawn.
    Each day
        another chance.

    II.

Tennessee Vital Records says, "Sharon Dawn."
Sharon, a "quiet and pretty" girl Mother knew
    in elementary school.

At first they spoke to Sharon.
It never occurred to me
    to answer.
She was so sweet and accommodating,
    she slipped down to S period,
        and then vanished altogether.
No one misses her,
    except the occasional telemarketer.

In defense of Sharon, my mother said,
    "Your father wanted to name you Ginger Dawn."
Ginger Dawn? Perfect,
    if I wanted to take my clothes off for a living.
This early reprieve created a karmic debt
    I may never sufficiently repay.

    III.

The last name, too, chafed
    over time.
Pinned to me by tradition,

my father's,
    father's,
        father's,
            father's,
                father's name.

Coppock.
A copse of trees
    all with but one legitimate branch.
Forks disregarded.
Women freely grafted,
    rootless,
        anonymous.
Chattel of the patriarchy.

    IV.

My mother's birth name:
    Martha n.m.n. Willison.
    No middle name.
First born of a patriarch so determined to maintain his strain,
    he was stingy even with her name.
After the cut and for always she would carry
    the recessive Willison.
Not trusted with a choice.

After his daughters married they were
    no longer of his house.
Even in death he said, "All to son."

    V.

Should I resist the name graft?
    I did.
Did I avert the transaction?
    I didn't.

I get the admonishing looks when he
    is wrinkled or mismatched,
the confirmation calls from his dentist.

Relations on both sides send warm holiday greetings
    to "Mr. and Mrs. David Seal."
I must seem in need of further pruning.
Who is this Mrs. David Seal
    whose mail arrives in my box?
The ironing board and crumb catcher must be hers.
Is it her job
    to tastefully coordinate my family's interiors?
    to cheerfully wipe my children's smudges with her spit?
If only she could collect the disapproval
    when I fall short.

    VI

And then my little Coppock-Seals,
    in copious springtime bloom.

    "Isn't it mean to make them write all that?"
    "What will happen when they marry?"
    "What if everyone did that?"

Often I answer," We could have given them
    just one name,
        but I didn't want to leave David out."

These same people look to me for the date
    of each child's last tetanus shot,
        criticize me when merit badges aren't promptly sewn.

He, of course, should not be expected to be
    the keeper of the trivia that is their lives.

To some, my name is a burden
    I foolishly bestowed.
Not knowing any better,
    my children accepted it like a gift.

They are rooted, connected, named and claimed
    by the guardian of their trivia.
The one who grew them like root vegetables
    deep inside herself.

    VII

I only regret that we cannot have
    all the names
        of all the mothers
            who fan out behind us
                like a richly embroidered train.

The women who loved us long,
    long before we were named.

At the Lorraine Motel

I stood on the time-line at the Civil Rights museum,
and looked both ways.

I've been to the Highlander Center,
on the minority recruiting committee.
I know all the words to "We Shall Overcome,"
and "Dixie."

I searched the pictures of the crowd outside
Dr. King's funeral for my father's face.
Daddy was there, just as baffled as I was
when Huntley and Brinkley showed the dogs,
the water hoses and school house steps.

*Just because of their skin, Mama? How can this
be just because of skin?*

My husband checks the angle from across the street,
pronounces the balcony a clear shot.

I am hit in front of a white robe in a glass case,
handmade with a woman's neat, small stitches,
familiar stitches, like stitches in my family's handwork.

I got my great-grandmother's unfinished embroidery,
the feed and sugar sacks, the mattress ticking.
I knew about her husband, on the Klan roll at the county library,
but I never thought about her patient stitches hiding him.

Who finally threw the damned thing out?
What became of the pattern?

Leo's Magic Pillow at the Fourth of July Picnic

A drab green plastic platoon is dug in
behind the blue throw pillow
Leo sits on to reach Aunt Jen's macaroni and cheese.
Barely enough hiney to hang his bright swim trunks.

He's wet from navigating a strip of aqua plastic
on the biggest hill in the yard,
the Crocodile Mile water slide,
SPF 40 for protection and speed.

Promising a magic show,
he produces an infantry soldier
from behind the pillow.
A skirmish of cousins ensues.

"You can't have him.
He's mine!"

You can't have him.
He's mine.

Dancing

Audrey
at 7
dances
like school's out and the ice cream truck is coming,
like playing in the water-hose with cousins.
Her body is mine
less 30 years.
Dancing as joy,
I vaguely recall.
Encumbered
even before
high school,
with sport,
fashion show,
mating rituals.
She grins and grabs my hands.
We spin and laugh. I twirl her around
like a ballerina on a mirrored box,
like every girl longs to be twirled.
I am, even with her,
self-conscious,
like that dream
of being naked
in a public place.
And yet
aware
that it is
as wrong
to seem
inhibited
as it is to be
ungraceful.
Audrey is neither.
Her body is still
her friend.

Star Wars

On the blue and gold pillow we share,
Luke raises his light saber with both hands.

Leo faces the wall,
my palm flat on his hard, thin chest.

Cold bleeds in from the pane of black
framed by a new window sash.

The old one blown out by a shotgun
over the heads of intruders two summers ago.

He is moving from fear to sleep.
Styrofoam planets sway with our breathing.

On Being Loved By Leo

He brings me treasure --
the blue, glass marbles
from spent spray cans
he and his daddy use
for target practice.

Waking to Violins

Stretching up
toward the sparkling surface of morning,
what is this, small and warm and burrowed-in
against my back? And violins?
Oh, yes, the clock radio and
my beloved.

Lightly, he cut in
while we were sleeping.
Just four, rolled into a tight curl.
The weight of my eyes
draws him up.
Oh, yes, his beloved.

Golden red hair,
time for a cut and morning wild.
Skin, softer than a breath.
I shine delight at him.
He kisses me.
This could be all and still
a windfall.

View from the Buggy

I try to stand between my daughter and the guy
two people behind us in line at Kroger.

He's tall and over-tan, in a stained white t-shirt,
holding a twelve-pack of Natural Light in one hand
and a Marlboro in the other.

She can't take her eyes off him.
I move to the left, she moves to the right.
I move to the right, and she stretches up to look over my shoulder.

Honey, it's bad manners to stare.
The woman behind us smiles politely.
Mama, he's smoking!
I move my lips to her little ear. *Shhh. Stop staring.*

He's going to die! She stage whispers,
poking her head between my body and my arm.
I want to watch.

She Thinks I'm Hard

She thinks I'm hard,
that I should move the kitten into the house.

Last year something -- maybe a fox --
got kittens on the screened porch.

She's twelve and from the suburbs,
a friend of my daughter's just here for today.

I tell her,
we coaxed that kitten in
from a culvert on the main road
where some soul sorrier than me
put it out.

My daughter keeps fresh litter in a box out there.
I buy cat food.

I do not say:
A fox is not a vegetarian,
and neither am I,
and neither are you.

No matter what I do, that kitten will die.
And the fox will die,
and I will die,
and you will die.

If she had any idea of the suffering
in every house on her tidy little cul-de-sac,
in my house,
in her house,
she wouldn't expect so much for a two-dollar cat.

At Eleven

My son is worried that time is accelerating,
that he won't be ready when his body is grown.

"It feels like my shoes are getting smaller
while my feet are getting bigger."

Yes, I say, *time does come in crazy fits and starts,
but still -- you can trust it*

*to ripen what's green.
Someday middle school will feel like too small shoes.*

"It's all too fast. I could do something bad."
But you won't, dear child. That very fear redeems you,

always with you, even when all you can hear
is the squealing of your own wheels.

The Size of Sadness

If it will stay small enough
to hold in one hand, cold,
gray, smooth as a river stone,
I can usually carry
most everything else.

Options for an Unplanned Pregnancy

In high school,
getting an abortion was a logistical matter.
In clumps along the corridors,
notebooks to new breasts,
we passed the hat, arranged rides, and alibis.

Now, I hold soft hands of sensible girls thinking of adoption.
Their mothers with dark, watery eyes
sit slightly behind,
aware of what their daughters are letting go.
The girls have no inkling
of the meaning of quickening.

Strangers to mother love --
that shoe-horn to the heart
that wriggles and wiggles
in slivers and bursts,
chest full of broken glass.

We talk about school, boys, money.
We talk about childcare and the future.
We look at pictures of smiling, childless couples
on their porches with red geraniums.

We are water striders
on a pool so deep
that the rock dropped now
will take years to hit bottom,
and ripple forever.

One day, in a house with red geraniums,
the stick will again turn blue.
The sweet birth mother will hug her husband
and talk about money,
about childcare, and the future.

And her second child will come.

And then she will know,
like a jackboot shattering her chest,
the bottomless grief of motherhood.

Cross Your Legs, Sweetheart

The gene pool wriggles with procreating slime.

Our sisters are sleeping
with men in ankle bracelets, for God's sake.
Stop trolling for whatever bites.
Keep the keepers.
Cut the rest off.

Does he hit women?
Hit the bottle?
Quit a job without a job?
Quit a job when he moves in with you?
Say it's your fault?
Say you look fat?
Call you his bitch?
Call 1-900?
Make fun of your dreams?
Make ugly scenes?
Neglect his mother?
Neglect to pay child support?
Come on to waitresses?
Come, and that's it?
Cheat on you?
Cheat with you?
Ask to borrow money?
Ask your cute friend to pile in?
Lie and it's not a happy surprise?
Lie on the sofa while you're at work?
Lose his driver's license?
Lose that bottle of pills from your broken arm last summer?

Cheaters cheat. Liars lie.
It's not what they do.
It's who they are.
For God's sake, Honey, throw that one back.

Photographs of Startled Men at McDonald's

Fathers signing adoption consents are skittish.
As the ink dries, I take a quick picture.
"You-don't-mind-if-I-take-a-photo-do-you?" *Snap.*

Some day his child will wonder
and the adoptive parents can say,
"Here, here he is. He was a McNugget man."

McDonald's,
McMerica's favorite rest area.
McMerica's garish branch office.

Even teenagers yet to master the condom
can find their way
to my McOffice.

Revised Standard Version

*If I then, your lord and Teacher, have washed your feet,
you also ought to wash one another's feet.*
　　　　　　　The Gospel of John 13:14

On my knees at the feet of an addict,
a new birth mother, still too sore to bend,
I, her lawyer, slipped on her Nikes,
carefully adjusted the laces, tied them.

Taking her home, I stopped
and bought her cigarettes,
an offering.

Waiving Grace

Below Exit 402 on I-40,
he signed away Grace.

Her father of genes and dreams,
fearing for his check, did not name her.

A Waiver of Interest.
Not much interest to waive,

really. Eleven years of unshouldered
expectation ended

with a lawyer,
trucks spraying dirty little tears.

To Grace's hesitant questions,
I answered,

her father signed
at "a meeting,"

and that he asked
about her.

I could not
tell her he signed

on my trunk lid,
under the interstate, in the rain.

Returning Joshua

Today the phone rang,
and four days of being
Joshua's parents stopped
in a hot church parking lot.

They raced to the hospital and held him
first. Named him.
Crying then, too.

Will he ever know
familial misfire,
snapshots of euphoria,
false starts on the road not taken?

They are wounded.
But his mother is bleeding.
Holding her joy like holding breath,
she clumsily straps him
into a new car seat.
Joshua is screaming.

"When the Lord takes,
he gives back in good measure, flowing
over," her mother says.
They've been shopping.

Strong and tall, he carries
the vacant baby seat and fist
full of tiny clothes
to a closet off the sanctuary.
His wife cannot look at them anymore.

Two Daughters Have Breakfast

This morning my Audrey sat in her high chair.
Whole grain panda puffs stuck
to her soft bib and cheek.

A daisy yellow sippy cup
of organic, happy-cow milk,
hand out for slippery slices of ripe banana.

This morning Brianna and her mom have been waiting for me
on the concrete lawn of the Union County Courthouse.
Her mother poured half her Mello Yello into the baby bottle

Brianna holds by the nipple. She toddles to us,
steadied by the standing ashtray,
hand out for more Skittles.

Mourning Prayer

Today there are too many to pray for.
The bright, red blood on the mouth
of a young possum dead on the shoulder of the road
finally wrenched the strong finger
from my infant grip.

Grasping at air,
I pray for myself.

Rx: Dirty Socks

He can't leave
his socks on the floor if
he has to wear them home.

Old Testament Man

I am not sad for you because
sometimes the Lord sends you frogs
and locusts, boils and gnats.
You trudge through, head down, bravely.
It's all there is to do.

I am sad for you because
once the Lord sent you a fawn-colored
woman with a pan of hot cornbread.
You walked on, barely raised your head,
as if it was all there was to do.

Be Bigger Than Me

Tuck me under your arm
like a midway prize.

Feed me pink cotton,
fleeting and sweet.

Tell me stories,
wild rides of neon and steel.

Lift me each time I reach up.
Sometimes I just want to feel small.

Regeneration

Newts, salamanders, skinks
wag shoulder to hip,
feet frantic.
The tail just follows.

Dam up the creek.
Tease them into coffee cans.
Soft, slick, enchanted.
Their capture costs them,
but they say the tails grow back,
like a charm.

Eye of newt, toe of frog,
lock of hair, soft little tail,
and pieces of heart. *Take it,*
take another little piece of my heart,
now, Baby.

Hearts, moons, stars, clover.
and diamonds, big blue diamonds.
Cross your heart and hope.
Cross your heart and tadpole promise.

Upon Meeting an Old Lover

Something about keeping you
at arm's length feels
like crumbling cornbread
into a glass late at night.

At first solid and whole,
but big palms cup my shoulder blades and
soft, beery lips press my forehead
to urge a giving way.

Pinch away the crusty edges first,
then press the tender middle
until there is nothing left to do but soak it
with buttermilk.

Winter Communion

First snow on my tongue,
face to the wind,
mouth wide,
breathing in
ice sparks bite cheek, lip, chin.
Wet and heavy,
some plummet
and burst.

How can a woman look
at something so bright,
so beautiful
and not want to take it
inside of herself?

Two by Two

Leaning, leaning, safe and secure from all alarms;
Leaning, leaning, leaning on the everlasting arms.

Written in 1887 by a couple of Presbyterians.
It figures.
That Presbyterian stiff upper lip, bear it, carry on.
This is what Deuteronomy offers Christians with no partner.
It falls a little short.

What a fellowship, what a joy divine,
Leaning on the everlasting arms;
What a blessedness, what a peace is mine,
Leaning on the everlasting arms.

Metaphorical arms just might work on Tuesday afternoon.
Rarely on Sunday morning sitting behind an old married couple.
She has a smudge of makeup on her collar.
He smells like Aqua Velva.
The sanctuary is sprinkled with widows, divorcees,
and women who have spit-shined kids
while their sorry men sleep it off.
These women want a real arm grazing theirs,
sharing the hymnal.

O, how sweet to walk in this pilgrim way,
Leaning on the everlasting arms;
O, how bright the path grows from day to day,
Leaning on the everlasting arms.

The song was written to comfort a new widower.
And it probably did, in the daytime.
But it wrapped his longing for two by two
in a shameful lack of faith.

In Genesis "The Lord God said,
It is not good that the man should be alone."
And it was not good --
beginning each day drinking coffee by himself.

*What have I to dread, what have I to fear,
Leaning on the everlasting arms?
I have blessed peace with my Lord so near,
Leaning on the everlasting arms.*

Let me wander through just one day

and float from shade to sun at will,
eat fried eggs when I get hungry,
draw in the porch dust with my toe.
In the picture I will look happy.

Advice from a Blue Heron

The middle of yourself,
move
from the middle of yourself.

Land without flapping.
Let the earth rise
to you.

The way I cock my head,
each long step,
pray like that.

Praise With Joy

I hold the open hymnal over his head.
He leans back against me
feeling me sing.
"Praise With Joy,"
page two hundred and seventy-three.

In the second verse
he convulses with laughter
like when I tickle his feet.
Pointing,
he prompts me to look.

A sparrow against
the sanctuary window.
Fluttering,
bobbing,
walking on the sill.

I smile at him and sing on.
Verse three and he's still laughing,
pulling my skirt.
I bend, ear to tiny lips.
"Look, Mama, he's dancing."

The Nature of Light

I
Who is it exactly, that comes in the spring?
Pressing forward like mint,
like new breasts,
like a week from Tuesday,
opening all of the boxes?

II
Halley's Comet returns in 2072.
Humans are 98.6 degrees, except sperm.
which are 98. nothing.
Without bees we would starve.
When is the next full moon?

III
The first thing Audrey said, after *more bites*
was that her name was Konowitz.
Audrey made her so mad we called her Skooter.
Before her, I didn't know a Konowitz.
Where was she then, and how did she get here?

IV
The David buckles tourists' knees. Every day
they fall right on the Carraran marble floor.
We sob for Romeo and Juliet at the ballet,
even without Shakespeare's words.
Who is this muse?

V
Leo wants a cookie.
Two of 'em he says, holding back one for his sister.
Mother grew them, but did not grow that.
What are these ties they find
while we are wiping jelly off the doorknobs?

VI
A broken a finger, the middle finger of a left hand,
split lengthwise from knuckle to knuckle.
Three weeks and not even a shadow on the X-ray.
I wonder,
why doesn't what breaks stay broken?

October on the Tennessee-North Carolina Line

It is mid-October and I am rich.
I throw back my head
and survey in slow rotation
great heaps of garnet and topaz,
emerald and citrine.
Jeweled facets snag the sun,
as it slips off an azure sky.
Rumpled vestments from the shoulders
of God Almighty.

The air too is rich.
Sandalwood and cedar,
moss and musk.
The crisp crunch of temporal death.

Economists are wrong, of course.
It is not the scarcity of gems
that give them value.
But our capacity for delight,
our willingness to be dazzled.
To see, after the green
is all gone and only essence remains
that we were always rich.

To Hold

Sarah and Phil are lawyers in D.C.
On 9/11, their two small boys were home
in Arlington with a sitter.
Impact created a gravitational pull
to family.
And the sitter would not stay.

The couple considers still their great good fortune:
Phil's Nikes at work.

Heels hobbled Sarah, but Phil ran.
Ran out of the city, across the bridge,
past the burning Pentagon,
through smoke and sprawl home.

A daddy in a suit and running shoes
crossing the Potomac.
That is an image to hold.

Small Game

We danced around you
yapping childish La-tee-das.
You lay in wait, on your back,

looking from face to face. We skipped,
giggling our edgy excitement.
Who would be the lucky, unlucky one

caught in the bear trap?
Finally, we tip-toed, knees high,
arms drawn up like little mice,

never knowing just how long we had.
Snap, your arm-jaws snatched a cub
and clamped it, an inescapable embrace.

The others, unable to wait, piled on,
a screeching, tickling, rolling heap.
This is how you captured us.

Walking the Farm Without You

>   in memory of Beldon David Colley,
>   and for David Lynn Seal

Here, this November, and for as long as I live
to remember, you
are the tie, the force binding
the protons and neutrons in this place.

Burnished red acorns,
red lacquered rose hips,
turkey wild as boys,
even the fescue in my shoes,

on this forty acres, you bind us all.
The smooth clay mud of the high pond
is imprinted by deer, who, like you,
I expect at the crest of each hill.

I will not remember ICU, overalls
limp and shabby, wrapped around underwear
on a plastic chair. I remember us

just this side of the fence line,
sharing a jar of ice water
under the biggest oak in the county,
after a fine day turning this very soil.

Statement of Faith

If you pay attention to a really good apple,
        each bite tastes different.
Being awake is very hard.
It took me thirty-five years to figure out I
am supposed to star in my life,
and that mean people are meanest to themselves.

There is no such thing as coincidence.
Religion is easy until you try to take it out and use it.
The Kingdom of God really is in our midst.
It's the love thing that trips most people up.
The family thing is the advanced course.

Reagan was right about one thing:
ketchup is a vegetable.
The 60's feminists got a couple of things wrong:
First, when they were burning lingerie, they missed the pantyhose.
Next, they only fought to take on more, and never to take on less.

Bar-be-cue transcends politics.
A big problem is nothing but a big pile of little problems.
If things are going to improve,
I must fill out the comment card.
Often, all I can do is disrupt the perception of consensus.

Stress comes from believing
things should be different than they are.
But the first real opening comes
when the status quo starts making us uncomfortable.
Wisdom is falling into paradox.

Prayer works as long as you let God define "works."
I believe in spirit guides.
Mine is a heron.
Not because I am like a heron,

but because I am not.

There are no grown-ups.
Crying is essential.
TV is a dangerous drug.
All princes are interchangeable.
Tea time is why there is no road rage in England.

Being a parent is, by far, the biggest ride in the amusement park.
Children need meaningful work, and so does everyone else.
It is unkind to insist children use their words instead of hitting
and then punish them for using the words
that are the best hitting substitutes.

Humor is not a trivial matter.
There is no place in an enlightened society
for artificial coloring, styrofoam or boxing.
What goes around really does come around.
Patience is revenge.

Either Disney or McDonald's is the Anti-Christ, maybe both.
Cool Whip is at least as scary as Freddy Krueger.
The only culture we have left for our very own
is what no one else wants.
That is why grits are so important.

The earth really is our mother,
and the moon is definitely a girl too.
Wild tastes like blackberries.
Sex smells like honeysuckle.
And I love

the owl and the pussycat
for dancing
by the light of the moon,
the moon,
they danced by the light of the moon.

Time

    Dear relentless

        accelerating blur

            all we have always

                lost.

Acknowledgments

"Advice from a Blue Heron" was originally published in *Wind*, the oldest independent literary journal in Kentucky.

Sincere thanks to Susan O'Dell Underwood and David Underwood for founding Sapling Grove Press out of their commitment to independent writers and visual artists. I feel extremely fortunate that this remarkable press believed in my voice and did such a lovely job editing and producing this book. Through their remarkable talents this book is so much more than the binder of dog-eared poems we started with.

I also thank my family, particularly my children, Audrey and Leo, for never complaining about their frequent appearances in these poems. Each person has a different take on the same circumstances. I appreciate my family graciously allowing my vision to inhabit its own space. Rick Held and Lissa Wood were patient copy editors, and along with Angi Cameron and all my dear girlfriends, my parents, and the French Broads were my stalwart cheerleaders. My thanks also to WDVX for putting poetry on air live every week. It is just one way the radio station lifts up local art and culture and enriches the Mountain South.

Dawn Coppock, December 2014.

About the author

Dawn Coppock has spent her career as an adoption attorney and an advocate for children. Her book *Coppock on Tennessee Adoption Law* is an essential reference for lawyers across the state. In recent years she has been entrenched in seeking a legislative end to mountain top removal coal mining in Tennessee, on behalf of like-minded Christians. Also active in the arts and writing community in the Mountain South, she reads her poetry regularly on the radio program *Tennessee Shines*, broadcast live from WDVX in Knoxville. She's the mother of Audrey and Leo, an award-winning pie maker, a proponent for Southern food and wild places, a yoga teacher and a gardener. She lives in Tuckahoe, Tennessee, which she'll tell you kindly is pronounced "Tucky-ho."